You Can Draw

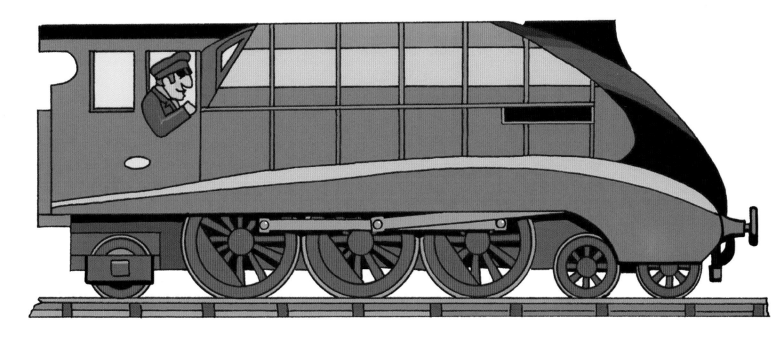

Trains

 **Gareth Stevens**
Publishing

Please visit our website, **www.garethstevens.com**.
For a free color catalog of all our high-quality books,
call toll free 1-800-542-2595 or fax 1-877-542-2596.

Library of Congress Cataloging-in-Publication Data

Bergin, Mark, 1961-
Trains / Mark Bergin.
    pages cm - (You can draw)
Includes index.
ISBN 978-1-4339-7478-6 (pbk.)
ISBN 978-1-4339-7479-3 (6-pack)
ISBN 978-1-4339-7477-9 (library binding)
1. Railroad trains-Juvenile literature. 2. Drawing-
Technique-Juvenile
literature. I. Title.
NC825.T7B47 2012
743'.896252-dc23

                                            2011049303

First Edition

Published in 2013 by
Gareth Stevens Publishing
111 East 14th Street, Suite 349
New York, NY 10003

© 2013 The Salariya Book Company Ltd

Editor: Rob Walker

Printed in China

CPSIA compliance information: Batch #SS12GS: For further information contact Gareth Stevens,
New York, New York at 1-800-542-2595.

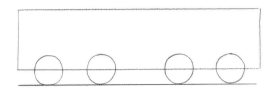

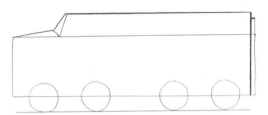

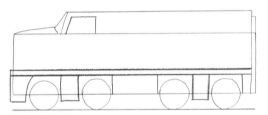

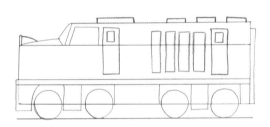

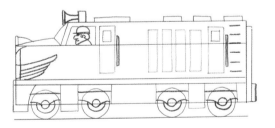

You Can Draw

Trains

By Mark Bergin

Contents

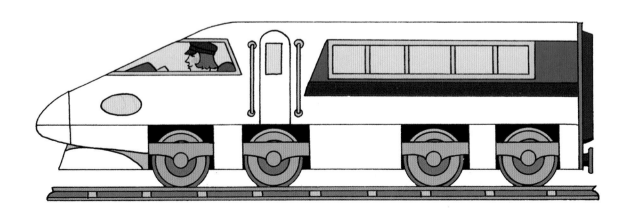

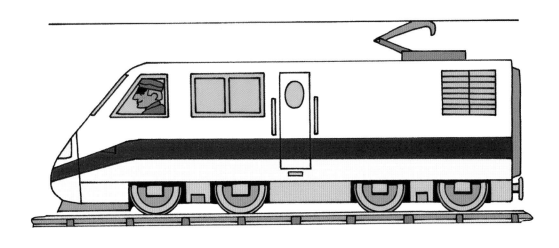

Introduction

Learning to draw is fun. In this book, a finished drawing will be broken up into stages as a guide to completing your own drawing. However, this is only the beginning. The more you practice, the better you will draw. Have fun coming up with cool designs, adding more incredible details, and using new materials to achieve different effects!

This is an example showing how each drawing will be built up in easy stages. New sections of drawing will be shown in color to make each additional step clear.

1

2

3

4

5

With practice, you too will be able to draw trains just like the examples shown here.

Materials

There are many different art materials available that you can use to draw and color your trains. Try out each one for new and exciting results. The more you practice with them, the better your drawing skills will get!

Use a pencil to draw in the shape of your train. Any mistakes you make can easily be erased, as can any construction lines that are left over at the end of your drawing.

Use an eraser to rub out any pencil mistakes. It can also be used to create highlights on pencil drawings.

You can go over your finished pencil lines with pen to make the lines bolder. But remember, a pen line is permanent, so you can't erase any mistakes!

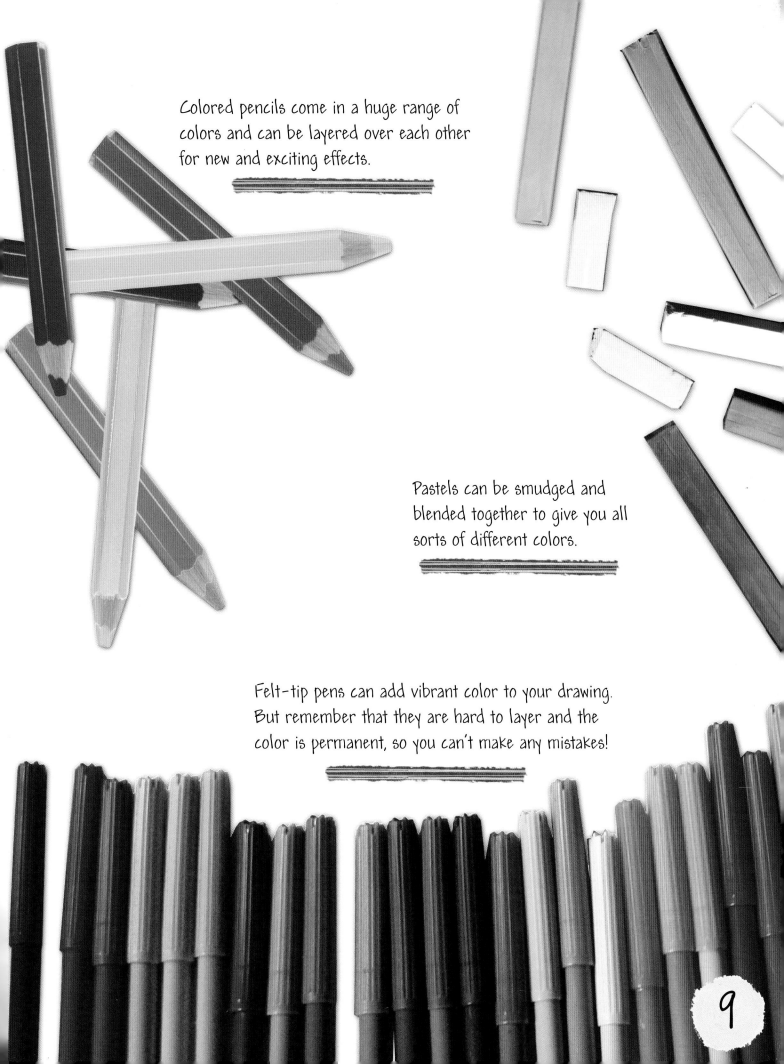

Colored pencils come in a huge range of colors and can be layered over each other for new and exciting effects.

Pastels can be smudged and blended together to give you all sorts of different colors.

Felt-tip pens can add vibrant color to your drawing. But remember that they are hard to layer and the color is permanent, so you can't make any mistakes!

Inspiration

There are many types of trains made throughout the world. You can choose any one of them as inspiration for your cartoon-style drawing. Look at photos, magazines, or books for new ideas and new designs to try.

When turning your train into a cartoon-style, two-dimensional drawing, concentrate on the key elements you want to include and the overall shape of the train.

One way to make your train look cool is to exaggerate its key features and perhaps add new ones!

Chose your own colors and designs to make your train look the way you want it to. It's your drawing, after all.

Stourbridge Lion

In 1829, the Stourbridge Lion became the first locomotive to operate in the United States.

Draw two circles for wheels and an overlapping rectangle for the boiler. Add a line for the track.

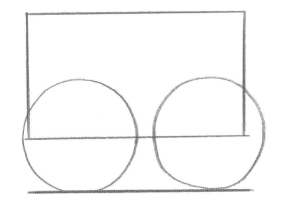

Add two inner circles to each wheel. Draw some straight construction lines through the wheels and add front and rear details.

Chimney

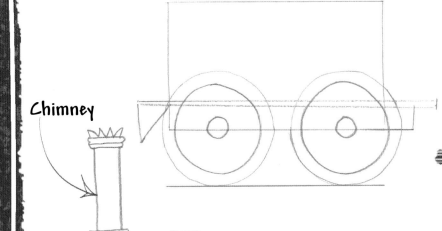

Add a tall chimney to the boiler. Draw in the extra details.

Pistons

Draw in the piston construction above the boiler and add pipes. Draw two smaller circles inside each wheel.

Draw in the driver. Add spokes to each wheel and a bar to connect both wheels together.

Spokes

Complete your drawing by finishing all the remaining details. Add puffs of steam and a rail track, and then color it.

Cog train

Cog trains are designed to climb steep slopes. They use cogs and racks to maintain grip when normal rails won't work.

Start by drawing two rectangles, one on top of the other.

Draw a triangular shape underneath and add four circles for wheels (one should be a smaller circle). Add a line for the track, and draw in the rectangle overlapping the wheels.

Draw in the windows and the door. Add the structure of the side panel.

Chimney

Steam dome

Add the chimney and steam dome. Draw inner circles on the wheels. Add the front bumper and detail at the rear.

Draw in the details of the wheel mechanism as shown. Add a whistle to the steam dome and draw in the driver.

Finish by drawing in the track and adding all the remaining details. Now color it.

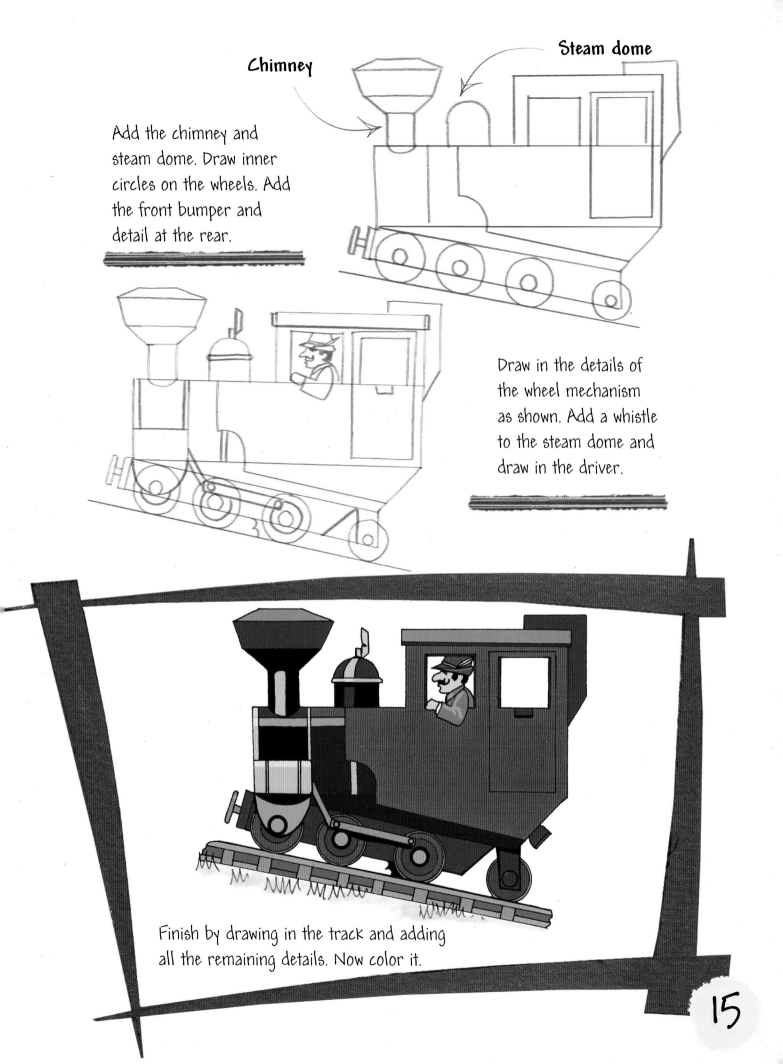

15

LNER Class A4

The LNER (London and North Eastern Railway) Class A4 were first built in 1935. Their streamlined design helped them to achieve record speeds for steam trains.

Start by drawing a very large rectangle. From left to right, draw two small circles, three large circles, then one small circle for the wheels.

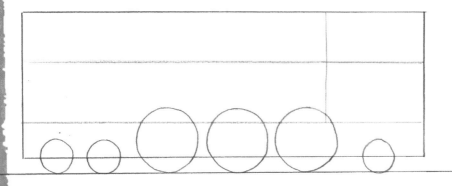

Divide the rectangle into sections (as shown).

Add the LNER's special curved front. Draw in the driver's cab.

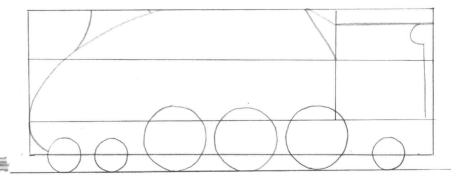

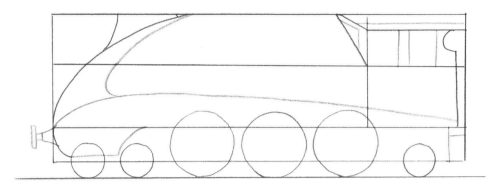

Draw in the streamlined design using curved lines. Add a front bumper and windows to the driver's cab.

Divide the body of the train into sections. Add the driver and carefully copy the wheel details.

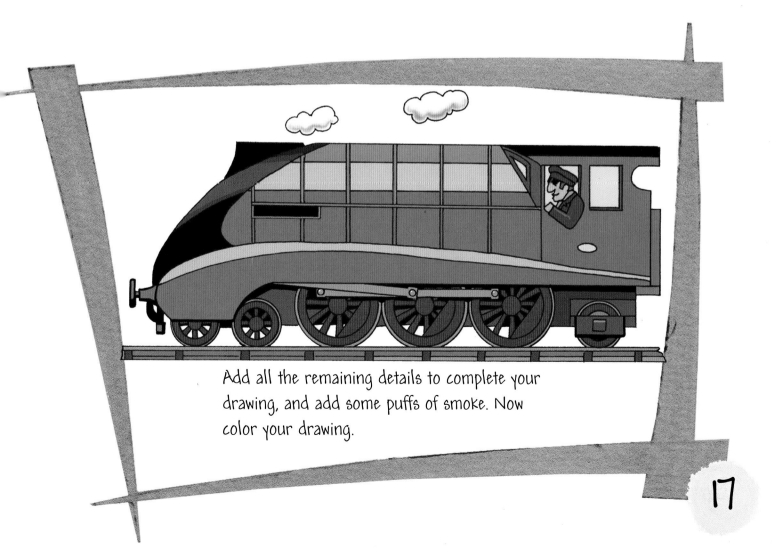

Add all the remaining details to complete your drawing, and add some puffs of smoke. Now color your drawing.

17

TGV

The TGV (Train à Grand Vitesse) is the French high-speed train. It is a great success and now runs through a number of countries in Europe. It can reach speeds of 200 mph.

Start by drawing a rectangle and a line for the track. Add four circles, with three of them overlapping the rectangle.

Curved nose

Draw in the curved nose of the train, and add a line running from the front to the back.

Draw in the windows, and add lines on either side of each wheel.

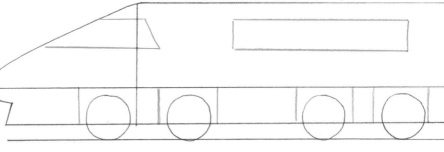

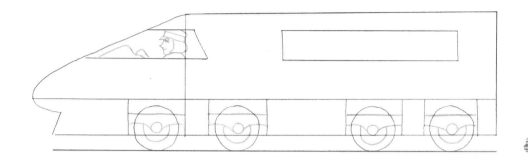

Draw in the driver. Add two more circles to each wheel and draw in the details of the wheel sections.

Draw in the door and rails, and add the window details. Draw in the rear coupling section.

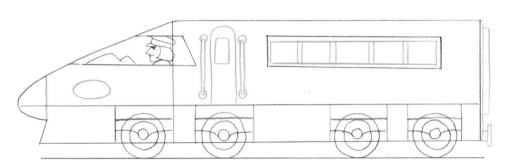

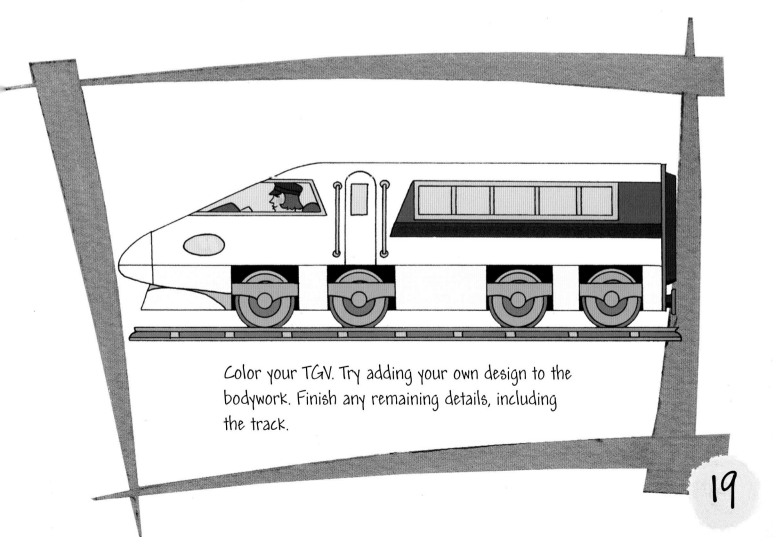

Color your TGV. Try adding your own design to the bodywork. Finish any remaining details, including the track.

Steam train

Steam trains use fire to boil water. This creates steam, which then builds enough pressure to drive the pistons that then turn the wheels.

Start by drawing in a rectangle. Add two large overlapping circles and two smaller circles for the wheels.

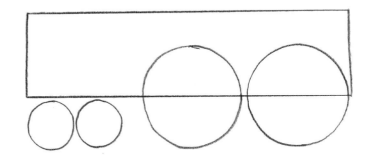

Draw in the driver's cab with two windows. Add another line below the rectangle that runs through the center of the smaller wheels. Add the track.

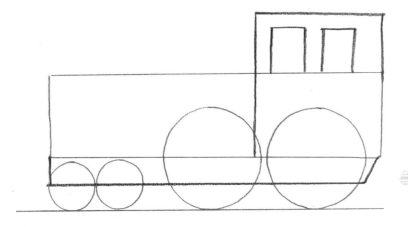

Cowcatcher

Draw in the cowcatcher at the front (the bit that removes debris on the tracks). Add a circle to each wheel and a line to the front window.

Chimney **Bell**

Draw in the chimney, the bell, and two domes. Add another small circle to each wheel and the curved front.

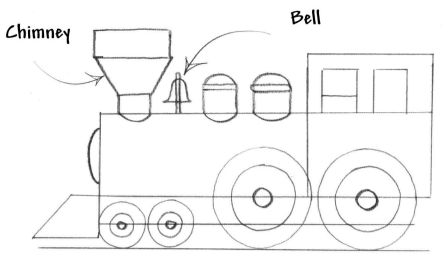

Lamp

Draw in the front lamp. Add the cab roof and the driver. Add detail to the cowcatcher, and then divide the main body into sections. Draw in the piston and the wheel spokes.

Finish your drawing by completing all remaining details. Color the body of the train and add some puffs of smoke.

Tank engine

Tank engines are compact and versatile types of steam locomotives. They can run in either direction at full speed.

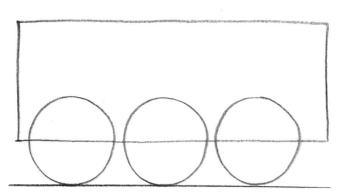

Start by drawing a rectangle. Add three overlapping circles for the wheels and a line for the track.

Draw in the driver's cab, and add windows and a door.

Draw in the sections of the main body. Add an inner circle to each wheel.

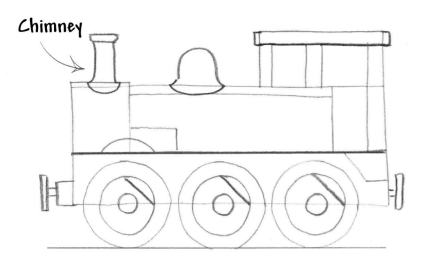

Chimney

Draw in the front and rear bumpers, chimney, dome, and roof. Add another circle to each wheel and a line (as shown).

Draw in the driver. Add spokes to each wheel, and draw in the connecting arms.

Complete your drawing by adding extra details like the track and puffs of smoke. Color your drawing.

Intercity-Express

The Intercity-Express train is Germany's fastest passenger rail service. It links most of the major cities and some beyond Germany, too.

Start by drawing a rectangle. Add four overlapping circles for wheels and a line for the track.

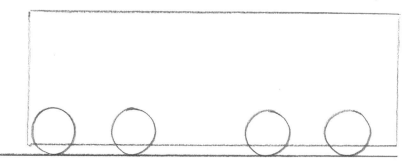

Draw in the curved front of the train. Add a line though the length of the rectangle section.

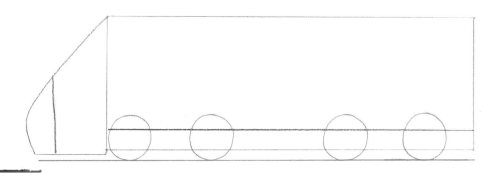

Vent Panels

Draw in the windows and vent panels, and divide the two sets of wheels.

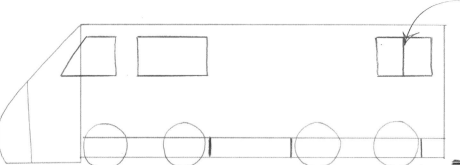

Add detail to the wheels. Draw another line through the main body, and add the coupling attachments at the rear.

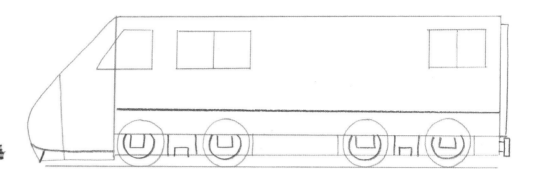

Draw in the driver and add a stripe to the train side. Add a door and vent. Draw in the electric cable above the train and the arm that connects to it.

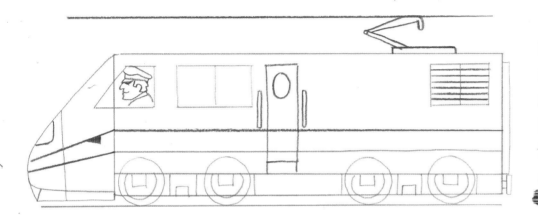

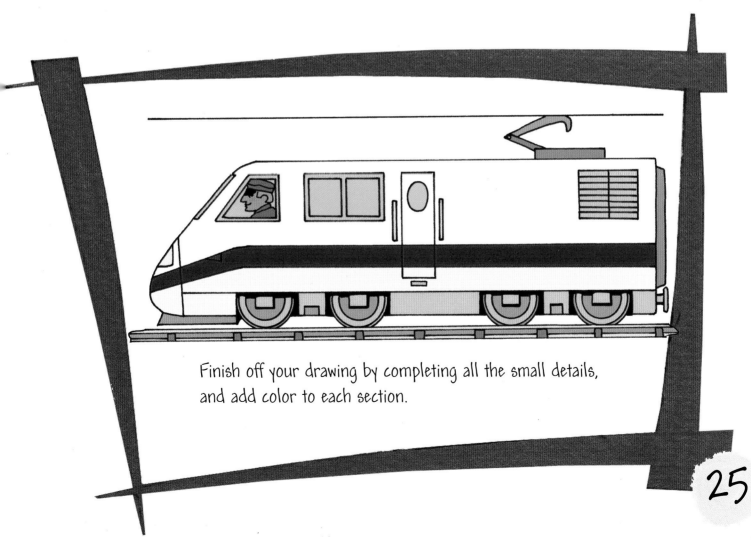

Finish off your drawing by completing all the small details, and add color to each section.

Diesel train

Diesel trains can carry their own fuel and run for long distances. They are useful for transporting goods or passengers.

Start by drawing a rectangle for the chassis. Add three circles for the wheels and a line for the track.

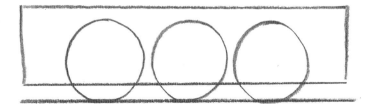

Draw in the main structure. Add a line across the top part of the wheels.

Divide the main engine into sections, and add the windows and the door.

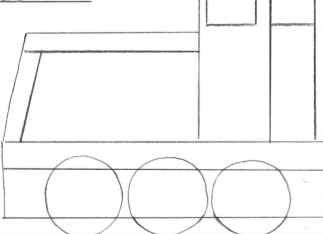

Bumper

Add front and rear bumpers. Add two more circles inside each wheel and connect them together as shown.

Exhaust

Vent panels

Draw in an exhaust, side panels for vents, a driver, and a handrail. Add spokes to each of the wheels.

Complete all the remaining details, and add color to your drawing.

Union Pacific

This powerful diesel train ran all over the United States delivering passengers, goods, and mail.

Start by drawing a rectangle, and add four overlapping circles for wheels. Add a line for the track.

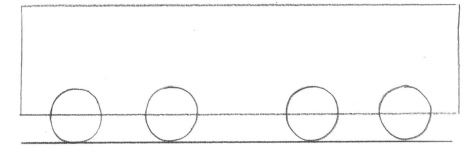

Using straight lines, draw in the structure of the train.

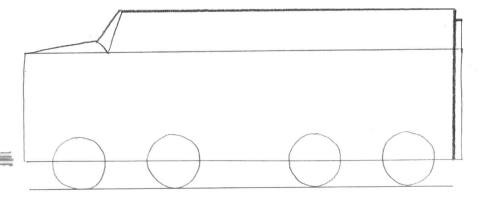

Draw in a window. Add new sections between the wheels.

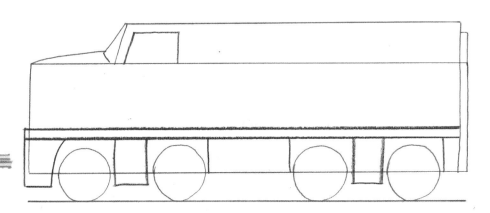

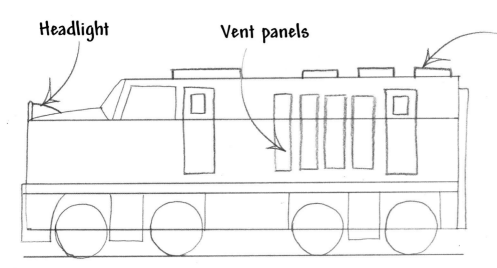

Headlight

Vent panels

Roof sections

Add the headlight and roof sections. Draw in doors and vent panels.

Draw in the horn on the roof, the paintwork design, and the door rails. Add the final details to the wheels.

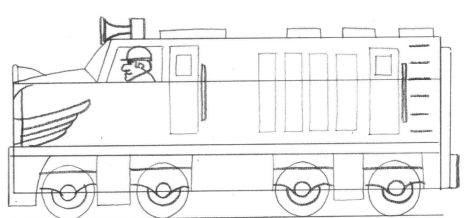

Complete your train by adding all the remaining detail. Then color each section and add a paintwork design. You can make up your own design.

More views

For an extra challenge, try drawing your trains from the front or rear! Practicing different views will improve your drawing skills.

Tank Engine

Front View

Start with a long, thin rectangle for the chassis. Add the main body with a curved roof.

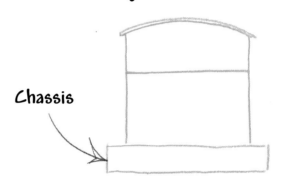

Chassis

Add circles for the windows and for the front view of the boiler. Add the chimney, wheels, and track.

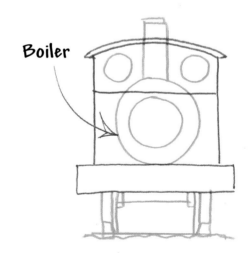

Boiler

Complete your drawing by adding small details like handles, bumpers, and couplings.

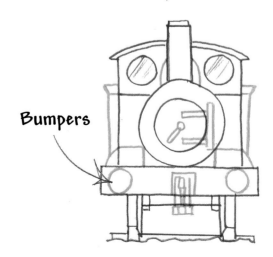

Bumpers

Back View

Start with a long, thin rectangle for the chassis. Add a box shape with two lines and a curved roof.

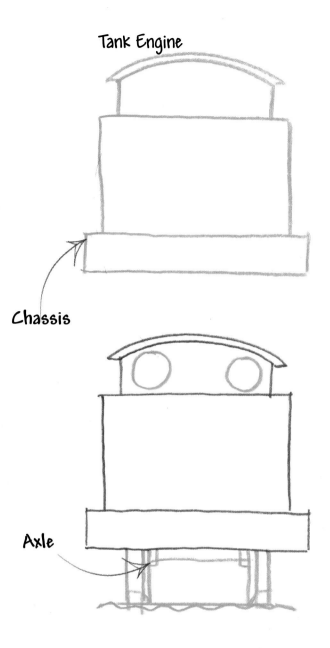

Tank Engine

Chassis

Draw in two circles for windows. Add the wheels joined with an axle. Then add the track.

Axle

Finish the drawing by adding the final details – the chimney, controls, bumpers, and coupling.

Glossary

axle A metal pole that connects the wheels across the bottom of the train.

bodywork The paintwork on the body of the train.

boiler The part of the engine that produces steam power.

cab The part of the train that the driver sits in.

chassis The frame at the bottom of the main body of a train.

construction lines Guidelines used in the early stages of a drawing. They are usually erased later.

coupling The parts of a train that link its separate sections together.

exhaust A pipe through which smoke from the engine escapes.

locomotive Another word for train.

piston A powerful, moving mechanism that helps to power trains.

steam dome The part of a train that separates steam in the engine.

streamlined Designed with smooth curves to reduce air resistance.

vent panel Panels at the side of the train that allow hot air to escape.

Index